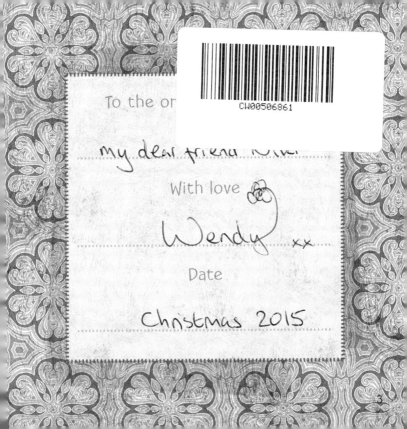

To the on

my dear friend Kiki

With love

Wendy xx

Date

Christmas 2015

CW00506861

3

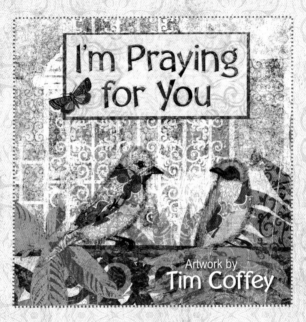

I'm Praying for You

Artwork by
Tim Coffey

HARVEST HOUSE PUBLISHERS
EUGENE, OREGON

I'm Praying for You

Text copyright © 2015 by Harvest House Publishers
Artwork copyright © by Tim Coffey

Published by Harvest House Publishers
Eugene, Oregon 97402
www.harvesthousepublishers.com

ISBN 978-0-7369-6396-1

All works of art reproduced in this book are copyrighted by Tim Coffey and may not be reproduced without the artist's permission. For more information regarding art prints featured in this book, please contact:

Courtney Davis, Inc.
340 Main Street
Franklin, Tennessee 37064
www.courtneydavis.com

Design and production by Garborg Design Works, Savage, MN

Harvest House Publishers has made every effort to trace the ownership of all poems and quotes. In the event of a question arising from the use of a poem or quote, we regret any error made and will be pleased to make the necessary correction in future editions of this book.

All verses are taken from The Message. Copyright © by Eugene H. Peterson 1993, 1994, 1995, 1996, 2000, 2001, 2002. Used by permission of NavPress Publishing Group.

All rights reserved. No part of this publication may be reproduced, stored in a retrieval system, or transmitted in any form or by any means—electronic, mechanical, digital, photocopy, recording, or any other—except for brief quotations in printed reviews, without the prior permission of the publisher.

Printed in China
14 15 16 17 18 19 20 21 22 23 / LP / 10 9 8 7 6 5 4 3 2 1

Splendor
and majesty
flow out
of him,
strength and
joy fill
his place.

1 CHRONICLES 16:27

FOR YOU I PRAY...

PEACE

Lord, may you fill my friend's heart
with peace. Give her the kind of
peace only you can provide—
peace that calms the soul, refreshes
the spirit, and restores balance.
She needs your peace to walk
faithfully into this day.
Thank you.

One single grateful thought
raised to heaven is the
most perfect prayer.

G.E. LESSING

GOD makes his people strong.
GOD gives his people peace.

PSALM 29:11

Peace like the river's gentle flow,
Peace like the morning's silent glow,
From day to day, in love supplied,
An endless and unebbing tide.

HORATIUS BONAR

Your peace is the foundation
from which we can reach for the
heavens. It is the source that
lets us love when we feel empty,
uncertain, or wronged.

HOPE LYDA

*May joy and peace surround you,
contentment latch your door,
may your troubles be less,
and your blessings be more,
and nothing but happiness
come through your front door.*

AN IRISH BLESSING

First keep the peace within yourself, then you can also bring peace to others.

THOMAS À KEMPIS

HEALING

Lord, please touch my friend with
your holy hands, and by your amazing
love give her the healing she needs.
I lift her—broken and bent from
walking the world's byways—up to you
to heal her body, mind, and spirit.
Thank you.

We are shaped
and fashioned
by what we love.

JOHANN WOLFGANG VON GOETHE

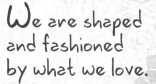

The Lord my pasture shall prepare,
And feed me with a shepherd's care;
His presence shall my wants supply,
And guard me with a watchful eye.

JOSEPH ADDISON

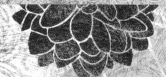

Those who needed healing, he healed.

LUKE 9:11

13

*E*verybody needs beauty as well as bread, places to play in and pray in, where nature may heal and give strength to body and soul alike.

JOHN MUIR

The soul is strong that trusts in goodness.

PHILIP MASSINGER

The very word "God" suggests care, kindness, goodness; and the idea of God in his infinity is infinite care, infinite kindness, infinite goodness. We give God the name of good; it is only by shortening it that it becomes God.

HENRY WARD BEECHER

LOVE

Lord, my friend is fearful and
disheartened. Please pour your life-
affirming love—the kind that chases
away all fear—into her life. And, Lord,
as she receives and revives, may she
understand that all good things come
from you. Every time. All the time.
Thank you.

The foolish fears of what might happen,
I cast them all away
Among the clover-scented grass,
Among the new-mown hay,
Among the husking of the corn,
Where drowsy poppies nod
Where ill thoughts die and good are born—
Out in the fields with God.

ELIZABETH BARRETT BROWNING AND LOUISE IMOGEN GUINEY

Courage is not the
absence of fear, but
the mastery of fear.

AUTHOR UNKNOWN

Jesus was quick
to comfort them.
"Courage, it's me.
Don't be afraid."

MATTHEW 14:27

God, when I feel afraid,
I will choose to trust in You.
JULIE K. GILLIES

Walk boldly and wisely in that light thou hast—
There is a hand above will help thee on.
PHILIP JAMES BAILEY

20

After a storm
comes a calm.

MATTHEW HENRY

Now God be praised,
that to believing souls
Gives light in darkness,
comfort in despair!

WILLIAM SHAKESPEARE

STRENGTH

Lord, my friend needs strength.
One thing after another has left
her breathless and dismayed. Lift
her chin, strengthen her faithful
stance, and then encourage her
to walk again with you. With you all
things are possible.
Thank you.

The harder the conflict, the more glorious the triumph. What we obtain too cheap, we esteem too lightly; it is dearness only that gives everything its value.

THOMAS PAINE

I'm with you. There's no need to fear for I'm your God. I'll give you strength. I'll help you. I'll hold you steady…

Isaiah 41:10

There is nothing as strong as tenderness, And nothing as tender as true strength.

Saint Francis de Sales

25

You can have hope in whatever your situation because He is a mighty and compassionate and loving God who will restore your soul. Hallelujah!

ELIZABETH GEORGE

Do not pray for easy lives. Pray to be stronger men. Do not pray for tasks equal to your powers. Pray for powers equal to your tasks. Then the doing of your work shall be no miracle, but you shall be the miracle.

PHILLIPS BROOKS

There is a sacredness in tears. They are not the mark of weakness, but of power.

WASHINGTON IRVING

FAITH

Lord, please bless my friend with unwavering faith. Help her rise above her messy moments and see each one from heaven's vantage. Then equip her with the knowledge and confidence to manage them in the way you would.
Thank you.

As well could you expect a plant to grow
without air and water as to expect your heart
to grow without prayer and faith.

C.H. SPURGEON

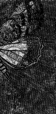

GOD rewrote the
text of my life when
I opened the book of
my heart to his eyes.

PSALM 18:24

As the body lives by breathing,
so the soul lives by believing.

THOMAS BROOKS

Where there is hatred, let me sow love.
Where there is injury, pardon.
Where there is doubt, faith.

SAINT FRANCIS OF ASSISI

*T*hank you that You care about the things I care about and that You understand my struggles even better than I do. Enable me to not only stay strong when I go through difficult situations, but to grow even stronger because I have put my hope in You and depend on You to bring me through it successfully. Teach me to always be watchful in prayer and growing stronger in faith.

STORMIE OMARTIAN

There is no love without hope, no hope without love, and neither hope nor love without faith.

AUGUSTINE OF HIPPO

32

*Weave in faith and
God will find the thread.*
AUTHOR UNKNOWN

33

WISDOM

Lord, as my friend makes decisions—
both big and small—she needs
wisdom from on high. As she kneels
before you, please gift her with that
gem of wisdom that helps her know
the direction you want her to go...
the way that leads to your blessing.
Thank you.

Honesty is the
first chapter
in the book of
wisdom.

THOMAS JEFFERSON

Tune your ears to the
world of Wisdom;
set your heart on a life
of Understanding.

PROVERBS 2:2

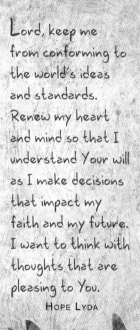

Lord, keep me
from conforming to
the world's ideas
and standards.
Renew my heart
and mind so that I
understand Your will
as I make decisions
that impact my
faith and my future.
I want to think with
thoughts that are
pleasing to You.

HOPE LYDA

Represent the Lord Himself as close to you and behold how lovingly and humbly He is teaching you. Believe me, you should remain with so good a friend as long as you can. If you grow accustomed to having Him present at your side, and He sees that you do so with love and that you go about striving to please Him, He will never fail you; He will help you in all your trials; you will find Him everywhere.

SAINT TERESA OF AVILA

Without courage,
wisdom bears no fruit.

BALTASAR GRACIAN

Those blessings are sweetest that are won with prayer and worn with thanks.

THOMAS GOODWIN

HOPE

Lord, you are the very wellspring
of hope. I pray you fill my beautiful
friend's heart, mind, and soul with
this precious gift today...and always.
Encourage her to kick off her shoes
and splash wildly in this great fountain
of possibility. Restore her hope in the
future and joy in the moment.
Thank you!

You're a fountain of cascading light, and you open our eyes to light.

PSALM 36:9

Never lose an opportunity of seeing anything beautiful, for beauty is God's handwriting.

RALPH WALDO EMERSON

Three grand essentials to happiness in this life are something to do, something to love, and something to hope for.

JOSEPH ADDISON

O man, believe in God with all your might, for hope rests on faith, love on hope, and victory on love.

JULIAN OF NORWICH

43

Hope keeps our
dreams alive.

JULIE K. GILLIES

For stars that pierce the somber dark,
For morn, awaking with the lark,
For life new-stirring 'neath the bark—

For sunshine and the blessed rain,
For budding grove and blossoming lane,
For the sweet silence of the plain—

For bounty springing from the sod,
For every step by beauty trod—
For each dear gift of joy, thank God!

FLORENCE EARLE COATES

Hope, like the gleaming taper's light,
Adorns and cheers our way;
And still, as darker grows the night,
Emits a brighter ray.

OLIVER GOLDSMITH

45

SERENITY

Lord, my friend sometimes says that her life seems too big and so hard. When she is overwhelmed, invite her to your side to lay it all down. Help her sort it out, pick up only the essential, and let go of the rest. Serenity—may this be your gift for her today. Thank you.

Young women will dance and be happy, young men and old men will join in. I'll convert their weeping into laughter, lavishing comfort, invading their grief with joy.

JEREMIAH 31:13

Mistake not. Those pleasures are not pleasures that trouble the quiet and tranquillity of thy life.

JEREMY TAYLOR

He has achieved success who has worked well, laughed often, and loved much.

ELBERT HUBBARD

The serene, silent beauty of a holy life is the most powerful influence in the world, next to the might of the Spirit of God.

BLAISE PASCAL

Is it so small a thing
To have enjoyed the sun,
To have lived light in the spring,
To have loved, to have thought, to have done?

MATTHEW ARNOLD

Depend upon it. God's work done in God's way will never lack God's supplies.

J. HUDSON TAYLOR

GRACE

Lord, because you are the grace-filled, forgiving One, I ask you to gently lead my friend to your cross and hear her whisper-soft heart's confession. And then, Lord, remind her of the way you see her—pure and lovely and beautiful in every way. Thank you.

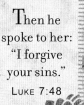

Then he spoke to her: "I forgive your sins."

Luke 7:48

The face is the mirror of the mind, and eyes without speaking confess the secrets of the heart.

Saint Jerome

God loves us unconditionally. His love
is available to each wandering heart. It
doesn't matter if you've wandered just a
few yards from Him or if you've ventured
far away. It's never too late to turn back
to God. That's truth. Believe it.

GWEN SMITH

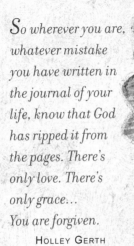

So wherever you are, whatever mistake you have written in the journal of your life, know that God has ripped it from the pages. There's only love. There's only grace... You are forgiven.

HOLLEY GERTH

I pray, O God, that I may be beautiful within.

SOCRATES

Forgiveness is the fragrance the violet sheds on the heel that has crushed it.

AUTHOR UNKNOWN

FRIENDSHIP

Lord, sometimes my friend is alone
and seems so far away. Please bless
her with loving friends to share a
good thought, offer an encouraging
word, enjoy a great big laugh, and
inspire a light-bright smile.
Thank you.

By friendship you mean the greatest love,
the greatest usefulness, the most open
communication, the noblest sufferings, the
severest truth, the heartiest counsel, and
the greatest union of minds of which brave
men and women are capable.

JEREMY TAYLOR

There is a comfort in the strength of love;
'Twill make a thing endurable, which else
Would overset the brain, or break the heart...

WILLIAM WORDSWORTH

A sweet
friendship
refreshes
the soul.

PROVERBS 27:9

One of the most beautiful qualities of true friendship is to understand and to be understood.

LUCIUS ANNAEUS SENECA

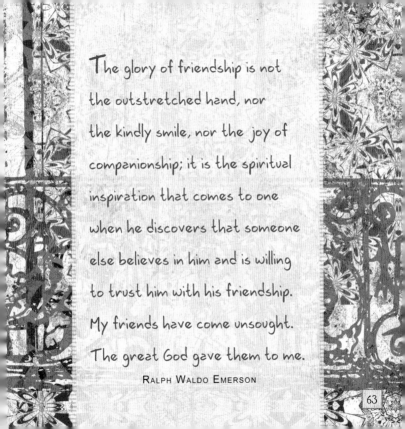

The glory of friendship is not the outstretched hand, nor the kindly smile, nor the joy of companionship; it is the spiritual inspiration that comes to one when he discovers that someone else believes in him and is willing to trust him with his friendship. My friends have come unsought. The great God gave them to me.

RALPH WALDO EMERSON

JOY

Joy! Lord, please fill my friend's heart
with joy! Thank you and amen.

You made me so happy, GOD.
I saw your work and I shouted for joy.

PSALM 92:4